To Nicole

How to be MOTIVATED all the time

Peter J Daniels

THE HOUSE OF TABOR

OTHER TITLES BY PETER J. DANIELS
How To Be Happy Though Rich
How To Reach Your Life Goals
How To Handle A Major Crisis
How To Have The Awesome Power of Public Speaking
Miss Phillips You Were Wrong

Tutorial programs:
Destiny
How To Get More Done And Have Time Left Over

All correspondence to:
World Centre for Entrepreneurial Studies
38–40 Carrington Street, Adelaide, South Australia 5000
Telephone: (08) 231 0111 Facsimile: (08) 211 8423

How To Be Motivated All The Time
Copyright © 1987 by Peter J. Daniels
National Library of Australia card number
and ISBN 0 949330 22 1

The author would like to thank Peter Haran for his valued assistance in the writing of this book.

Printed by Australian Print Group
Victoria, Australia.

Published by **The House of Tabor**
  84 Northgate Street,
  Unley Park, South Australia 5061.

The best antidote to
discouragement is motivation.
A person who is both personally
and permanently motivated
doesn't give up easily!

To Dr. John Haggai whose
motivational uplift does more for
people than any man I know.

Contents

Preface

I could just hear what they were saying as they came up into our apartment. Greetings were exchanged and our visitors were evidently looking through the glass doors into the lounge room observing me stretched out on the lounge with my eyes closed. One of the guests said to my wife Robina, 'Isn't it nice to see Peter resting? I don't think I have ever seen him like that before.'

My wife responded, 'Don't you believe it, he's not resting, he's probably working very hard at something — he's motivated all the time.'

Later our guests asked the question: 'Is it possible to be motivated all the time?' I responded with a resounding 'Yes!!'

As I have moved around the world speaking to groups of people from many nationalities the question usually arises, 'How can I be motivated?' or, 'How can I motivate someone else?' or, 'Can I have motivational permanence?' While it is true that motivation — or lack of it — comes to us all at times, it is generally triggered by an outside force or influence causing us to respond. These forces can involve threats, fear, crisis, conflict, love, hate and anger. But just as these can motivate us they can also destroy us if they are not brought under control and programmed through discipline and planning.

Can you actually program motivation? I believe you can. Furthermore I believe you can do it in such a way that it remains a permanent part of your work and personality.

Doctor John Edmund Haggai, to whom I have dedicated this book, remains to me the most motivated individual of our time. Consistently he is on the move, carefully but swiftly gliding through life like some graceful mental ballerina, with a minimum of fuss and a maximum of results. His manner is always pleasant, his objective always clear and his resilience, even in the most awesome of situations, is prompt and accurate. Someone once said of John Haggai that after fifteen minutes with him you feel you can conquer the world.

Is this just psyching yourself up or being puffed up with an unnatural ego? Is it just arrogant verbal boasting? No, I believe it is much more than that. It is a way of life that exudes confidence and produces the final product whatever that may be. And inspires all those who become involved to creative and purposeful action.

W. Clement Stone, the famous insurance tycoon, at 85 years of age exudes this quality. He attributes his rise from humble beginnings to this motivated attitude. And he has inspired millions by his life.

I hope this book will give you the formula to help you to be motivated all the time and propel you to achievement you never dreamed possible. Read this book many times and underline and emphasise — by involvement — those principles that particularly appeal to you. Make them a part of your personality by initiating habit force and through the repetitive process make it your very own.

At the end of our lives we are going to look back on our time spent on this planet with reflection, insight and hindsight. Most of us will have some regrets and we will see areas that we could have improved upon. But let us try. Let us be motivated to have a go. Let us give life our best shot by being honest with the breath that God has given us and respond to the opportunities and oppositions presented by accepting and demonstrating to others 'How To Be Motivated All The Time'.

Peter J. Daniels

Motivation is Deeply Personal

You must accept that you can change and that a pattern of principles adhered to and used repeatedly will not only direct your life, but change it permanently.

CHAPTER ONE

Motivation is Deeply Personal

Many people think that motivation just happens, that some are born with it and others are not.

While it may be true that some individuals are more outgoing and aggressive than others, it is also true that motivation, like any behavioural science relationship, can be learned.

My own story is an example of that. I am basically an introvert. I would far prefer to spend time alone or with a few people than participate with a crowd or lead a parade. But my frustration at seeing problems that needed a solution and opportunities that should be grasped clearly showed me I needed to get motivated to get the job done and to maintain a continual momentum towards a predetermined goal.

Motivation is not something caught like a common cold. You may pick up the enthusiasm of it if you are in the company of a highly motivated individual, but it will disappear quickly if principles are not learned and objectives are not clearly defined. Nobody can get inside your mind and body and act it out for you. Your motivation must come from within, and the first principle of motivation — as in any change of behaviour — is *to want to change and have a very good reason for doing so.*

Most people who speak to me at seminars or in private desperately want to be *motivated* but have very shallow reasons for wanting to *change.* Some think it is just a matter of acting it out and everything then falls into place. Nothing could be further from the truth. When the first real calamity or crisis strikes, the acid test begins. It is at these times that you are thrown back on the principles you have adopted. You must test them, as it were, in the heat of battle. Under such pressure your motivation is proved. In a crisis situation the cliches go, egos deflate and actors forget their lines. That is why principles of life in all areas must go through the fire of battle to prove their value.

Motivation in its very early stages is an act of discipline and you will find it will need to become more and more a part of your personality. Motivation actually determines your lifestyle because it relates to the things you do both in work and leisure. It also determines the direction which you follow in business and even politics. A highly motivated person wants to see things accomplished and is prepared to pursue an objective with vigor in his or her value system that presents a worthy challenge. Motivation does not mean 'at all costs' or 'at any quality'. Quality and quantity of life have a binding partnership with growth.

Your new motivated lifestyle will act as a magnet to others and draw them towards you because they hope somehow to obtain what you have and be part of that inspirational package. As you draw others, take care not to allow them to drain your energy and time. Do not abdicate your own objectives and principles and end up redundant.

You must accept that you can change and that a pattern of principles adhered to and used repeatedly will not only direct your life *but change it permanently.*

A friend of mine who was extremely shy and in need of motivation forced himself into a situation that changed his life permanently. Allan was a country boy who suddenly found himself surrounded on a College campus by other young people, who had bright and outgoing person- alities. He always seemed to find himself on the back burner waiting for something to happen. Of course it never did.

Brooding on the situation, he decided he had to change. He was going to be motivated and popular, but he first needed a plan to bring about that change. This is what he did.

First, Allan had cards printed with his name, room number and other items of interest on them. Then he met every bus or car that brought new students to the College and helped them with their bags, showed them the facilities and invited them to contact him if they needed any further assistance. Then he gave them his card.

The results were fantastic. Allan not only motivated himself into action, but by careful planning drew literally hundreds of others toward him, and was a great help to them in the process.

Why not make a decision today, this moment, to repeat and persevere with the principles and suggestions in this book? Move up to a level of living and achieving by becoming highly motivated. Recognise that motivation is deeply personal and that it can only be achieved by making it a daily part of your very existence. Hunt down those areas of your life that are negative, critical and suspicious and replace them with positive thought and action as well as praise and trust in others.

I find it interesting that the Bible is full of optimism, positive thinking and affirmation. It was here my first love for personal motivation was born. As I read continually through its pages I am amazed as it unfolds the ultimate in motivation. This is clearly demonstrated by Jesus whose face was as flint when He journeyed to Jerusalem, unswerving in His commitment to release all mankind from the bondage of sin and open the way for all to the wonderful mystery of eternal life.

You can become a positive, optimistic and motivated person if you want to.

It cannot be permanently imposed from without, but *must be permanently created from within*. You will notice the change almost immediately and soon you will hear comments from others which will confirm that change.

Make the commitment, follow the principles in the following chapters and keep short accounts of your progress. This will ensure that you do not slip back into the old ways, but rather progress with each new day. As you ponder the fruits of motivation just imagine what you would be like without it — dependent on others, lethargic, fatalistic, lazy, negative, unimaginative, dull, frustrated and failing. All you have to do is *reverse* each of these impositions and you will find you will become self confident, energetic, full spirited, optimistic, positive, imaginative, exciting, objective and successful.

MOTIVATORS
- Only you can act out your motivation.
- Motivation determines your lifestyle.
- Motivation creates new relationships with others.
- Motivation is a disciplined personality.
- Motivation is your best *you*.

CHAPTER TWO

Have Clearly Defined Boundaries

Having clearly defined boundaries will put you light years in front of your competition and make life itself easier and less complicated.

Have Clearly Defined Boundaries

I would point out here I am not advocating limitations of choice. But I am suggesting you make right choices. Consider firstly areas of preference and stick with the decisions you make.

It is quite obvious, because of limitations of energy, time and finance, all the things that need to be done in this world cannot be done by one person. But do not let that limit your growth.

The bottom line is that you cannot do everything but you can do something! So why not make deliberate careful choices within your sphere of influence and stick to them permanently — or at least until you have run your full course?

You cannot be motivated if you want to do everything, be everywhere and control all things. *Energy must be directed and channelled into specific areas.* Concentration of thought and imagination must also be carefully directed to provide the motivational stimuli. For example, I would dearly like to become involved in music but I cannot, because it would mean a dissipation of imagination, thought, time and energy that I would have to drag away from those areas demanding my full motivational thrust.

Be selective and measure all involvement against your availability of time, finance, energy and imagination.

There is some truth in the saying that if you want anything done you should give it to a busy man. You can accept or take in all kinds of quite worthwhile and rewarding tasks that give you satisfaction and results. But the criteria must be whether it will fit into your choice of commitment areas where your motivational thrust is available.

I am continually pursued by people and organisations who want me to become involved and do all kinds of wonderful and not so wonderful things. But because I have life goals (see next chapter) and have accepted limitations by personal choice, I can easily and quickly assess whether or not what I am asked to do fits into my motivational energy and commitment area.

Why not now list those areas in which you are not prepared to become involved, either polit-ically, socially, financially, morally, geograph-ically or physically. Keep that in a book, carefully dated and updated as more areas come to mind.

Some years ago I made a list of people I had helped over a twentyfive-year period who had not responded to my assistance by acknowledgement or by helping themselves and others. I checked that list out and in one day took more than seventy people out of my life forever. It seemed to me at that time foolish to spend a part of my life encouraging, uplifting and financially supporting people who never responded to my help. The fact was that continuing to help them prevented me from assisting those who were anxious to respond and grow.

I have now a written criteria for involvement and help, along with a time frame for results and my motivational thrust is no longer wasted in that area. The relief I experienced by taking that action with those seventy people was enormous. It freed me up for new time and talent opportunities which increased my motivation and released a new enthusiasm for getting things done.

After you have made your list of preferred areas of involvement for life, watch out for saboteurs. It may be at a social gathering or a quick phone call that you will find you have suddenly committed yourself to a scheme or venture outside of your preferred area. You may not realise what has happened until sometime later. A foreign commitment demands motivation. It must come from somewhere. So you rob other projects of your attention thereby minimizing your effectiveness. Be very careful during these times not to get caught up with pseudo-rationale which allows

−your subconscious to rationalise the involvement or commitment that breaks down the boundaries and puts it into your preferred area. Our subconscious will continually play tricks on us if we do not seek truth, discipline and commitment within our clearly defined boundaries.

Care needs to be taken to examine regularly our commitment and involvement so we do not allow intrusion into our preferred areas. To be motivated all the time we must reassess our boundaries regularly for saboteurs. Sharpen the definition for your boundaries frequently because in so doing you are evaluating your life, *and the more you evaluate your life the more selective and directive you will become.*

Having clearly defined boundaries will put you light years in front of your competition and make life itself easier and less complicated. Decisions will prove to be less complicated and difficulties and personality clashes will be reduced. It is an enjoyable and exhilarating life knowing those areas you have chosen to be involved in. Your energy, your spiritual, physical and mental attitudes are then directed to your choices. Some people may not understand and others may envy you, but all will notice what you accomplish and the motivational spark that exudes from you.

A final word of caution in regard to your boundaries. You will generally find that diversions come in two distinct forms.

1. The silent commitment that evolves slowly until suddenly you wake up to find too late it has a grip on you.

2. The one that looks lifelike and seems a unique and profitable opportunity. In one great lapse of conscience you drop your defence and welcome it in, ignoring all the reasoned judgements of your list of preferred and committed tasks.

Motivation is your life's blood towards continued achievement. *Do not allow it to be wasted by an intrusion of any kind.* Have clearly defined boundaries and protect them well.

MOTIVATORS

- You cannot be motivated if you want to do everything — be selective.
- Boundaries are not limitations, they are selected choices.
- Do not allow intrusion into your preferred areas — otherwise you will diminish thrust.
- Reassess your boundaries for saboteurs.

CHAPTER THREE

Have Long Term Goals

When you make a long term goal, you are declaring to your mind, body, and spirit that all forces are in tune together and come what may, it will be done — no back down, no defeat, no retreat.

CHAPTER THREE

Have Long Term Goals

In my book *How to Reach Your Life Goals* I examined the premise that goals should be for life.

The constant stream of letters and phone calls I receive from around the world indicates that message has struck home. All major achievers in any field of involvement are long term goals setters. That is not to say that they do not set short term goals — they do, but only as a filling or progressive step towards the ultimate goal.

A permanently motivated person has long term goals *because long term goals ensure motivational permanence.* If you really are serious about developing a lifestyle of motivation then now is the time to look into your long term goals program for security and direction.

Psychologists and behavioral scientists have never been able to explain fully what happens to us when we commit our lives to worthy goals. History abounds with stories of remarkable achievements in all fields that were realised by an individual whose motivational thrust was akin to something supernatural. But careful examination will show that the motivation was an out working of a long term passionate goal.

When you make a long term goal you are declaring to your mind, body and spirit that all forces are in tune together and come what may it will be done — no back down, no defeat, no retreat. A commitment of that magnitude cannot help but push your very being into a motivational stance that almost defies description.

Most people think and dream in the area of fantasy, hoping and expecting that somehow, some day, maybe those dreams will materialise. *Long term committed goals turn fantasy thinking into fantastic thinking, because they represent reality and action.* While you fantasise, you are programming yourself to be content in the unrelated world of wishful thinking. But fantastic thinking takes a hard firm grip on reality, nailing down principles and procedures.

Having a long term goal provides a catalyst for motivation at every waking moment. All your senses are committed to a specific task and turned to a sharp focus; your motivational thrust is excited because it always has a track on which to run. Often I meet and talk with some great achievers. The interesting thing to me is that people at ages long past retirement maintain their motivational edge because of their long term commitment. That can happen at all levels of society.

I firmly believe that a long term goal, committed to in totality, and programmed with time frames can actually reprogramme your body clock and increase your life span as well as prolonging good health. Many people who move into a retirement situation (particularly men), without adequate provision for a long term commitment are not long for this world.

My years of successful real estate involvement have shown me an indisputable pattern. Moving to a much smaller home and removing the commitments of daily life and struggles are sure signs of life termination. It is a sad but true fact. Why not programme your body clock far past the normal years of retirement with a commitment now to a life goal which will stretch and grow and achieve until the end of your days?

The simple principles of goal setting are as follows:

1. *Clearly define your goals.*
2. *Set out your strategy.*
3. *Plan out the problems.*
4. *Build in reserves.*
5. *Relate everything to a time frame.*
6. *Create a master plan for achievement.*
7. *Action — do it now.*[1]

No one can vigorously pursue a lifestyle of motivation without receiving in return some sort of satisfaction. Short term goals very often give a rush of energy and excitement until the finish line.

But there usually is a let down after the prize has been won. Long term goals prolong satisfaction because in an expandable goal, minor and major achievements are met within timeframes. They form an intrinsic and important part of the whole long term goal.

Life achievers are never satisfied with the status quo or even a major achievement. No, they press on even further after they seem to have reached the pinnacle and amaze us all with their higher achievement. What is their secret? It is really quite simple. They get their satisfaction out of being dissatisfied with present and past performance, because they know they can always do more and do it better. I call it *inspirational dissatisfaction*, and used wisely and positively it creates potent motivation and achievement.

Make long term goals a part of your life's commitment and experience the exhilaration and the warmth of being motivated all the time.

MOTIVATORS
- A goal for life ensures motivational permanence.
- Long term goals create commitment.
- Long term goals turn fantasy thinking into fantastic thinking.
- Long term goals can actually reprogram your body clock.

1. For a comprehensive study of goal setting with formulas, see my book *How to Reach Your Life Goals*.

Develop a Positive Mental Attitude

A positive mental attitude means spending your creative energies on finding ways things can be done rather than exhausting your emotional and mental powers dwelling on the way things cannot be done.

CHAPTER FOUR

Develop a Positive Mental Attitude

Here is a simple principle for developing a positive mental attitude: Look back at all the fears and negativity in your past life and note how futile they were. Wouldn't a more positive lifestyle have changed every situation for the better? The Christian charter calls it faith. In fact, the Bible quite clearly states that 'all things work together for good for those who love God' (Romans 8:28).

A positive mental attitude is an act of faith, accepting, hoping and working toward a good result in every situation. A positive mental attitude is constructive and affirming, while a negative mental attitude is destructive and unsettling.

How often has this happened to you? You have a good idea, you develop and investigate it, and become excited about its possibilities. Then you share it with someone else only to receive a negative response. All the excitement collapses and fades!

In a business meeting, how often have you let the dissenters become the deciders and allowed great thoughts, dynamic dreams and future plans to become nullified by a negative brick wall? Negativism is powerful because it has locked within its framework the threat of fear, doom, gloom and calamity and requires us generally to do nothing.

Have you ever noticed how a negative action controls a situation? Phrases like 'I'm not sure about this project', or, 'If we do this, there could be real problems', or, 'This is going to cost a lot' stun us to silence, even though they are very often not followed by fact. Is it any wonder that a positive mental attitude is so hard to develop but so welcome to find?

A positive mental attitude means spending your creative energies on finding ways things can be done rather than exhausting your emotional and mental powers dwelling on the ways things cannot be done. It means turning a problem into a solution. It means you must develop what we call thought displacement.

Let me explain a little further. Maybe you have a negative thought in your mind and it is nagging and pulling you down. What is really happening is that you are focusing on the thing you do not want to happen and in doing so you are, in a sense, majoring on the catastrophe and not the solution.

Thought displacement changes all that; but *it requires discipline and imagination.* Let's get down to nuts and bolts.

Firstly, write down ten things that you would *prefer* to happen. This may seem an incredible task. But once you start to use your imagination you can do it. For instance, you may prefer to spend time at the beach, visit friends, go to a movie, have dinner at a nice restaurant, help someone in need, earn more money and so on.

Write these down and expand upon them. When you finally have them all documented, read them aloud at least twenty times and then imagine and think about the solution to the negative problems you have. Force yourself to think only of the solution. When the negative thought returns, challenge it and replace it with a solution.

Secondly, when I find a negative mental attitude prevailing, I try to flush it out by reading the life stories of people who have overcome incredible difficulties. In so doing I can positively relate to the fact they not only survived but went on to win.

Thirdly, I might 'scare' it out by doing something that requires all my mental and physical resources, like riding a difficult horse. I find my mind and body refreshed by the experience.

Another principle I use is to read aloud daily an affirmation sheet that tells me clearly who I am and what are my relationships, my responsibilities and my life goals. With this daily check I keep positive and highly motivated.

What we have to be very careful of in developing a positive mental attitude is allowing our subconscious mind to take us off the right track. Quite often we may not feel motivated or positive, but if we act and behave motivated, our minds and spirits will respond.

Somebody, somewhere will do what you want to do. They may have already done it, so why not you? The only real difference in high achievers and highly motivated individuals is their attitude. Your *attitude* determines your *altitude* in life.

Look for the positive in every situation. If you do you will definitely find opportunities for growth, learning and experience.

Avoid such phrases as:

I'm not sure
I can't do it
It will not work
I may fail
It's a problem
It will wear me out

Rather use affirmations like:

I'll find out
I can do it
It will work
I will succeed
It's an opportunity
It will help me grow

Remember the principles of the previous chapters about goals and preferred areas and take the principles of this book as a whole in working out a pattern of behaviour that you can apply daily.

MOTIVATORS

- Believe that most things can be done by someone — why not by you?
- Act physically motivated and you will be mentally stirred.
- Develop thought displacement.
- Use a daily affirmation sheet.
- Don't let your subconscious take you along a path you do not want to go.

Develop a Deep Personal Integrity

Why not be someone you can admire yourself? There is absolutely nothing wrong with that. As a matter of fact, the Bible says quite clearly you should love others as you love yourself.

CHAPTER FIVE

Develop a Deep Personal Integrity

Whether we do so consciously or unconsciously, we all adopt a level of integrity in our business and personal lives towards others. In other words, have reasonably clear ideas of integrity as to what we will or will not do. In any given situation an assessment can be quickly made as to the integrity of the project or involvement without a great deal of anguish. Rarely would we break a commitment in business or personal life towards others. However, that really does not demonstrate our real integrity quotient.

If you are having difficulty in staying motivated all the time, examine closely your personal integrity. Root out past and present commitments you have made and ask yourself the question, 'Would I treat another person with the same level of integrity I display towards myself?'

My guess is that we treat other people with much more commitment and integrity! Why should we not have integrity towards ourselves of the same measure at least as we give others?

One of the major reasons we do not remain motivated all the time is we do not retain integrity towards ourselves in the same measure as we do towards others.

Highly motivated people are those who keep commitments to others, but who also keep commitments to themselves. That is why they always look and sound so confident and why they achieve and keep on achieving.

Try this simple exercise. Why not find a person, either living or dead, to whom you can relate, someone you can hold in high esteem. Examine carefully what it is about that person that you admire so greatly.

If the person is deceased, read all you can about his life and examine the areas you admire.

In the case of living persons you may even be able to take them out to lunch and ask them questions.

Observe first hand their mannerisms and thereby create a profile that you can emulate. Pick out specific good points you would like to adopt and practise them daily. In this way, you can develop the good and admirable qualities you see in others.

Why not be someone you can admire yourself? There is absolutely nothing wrong with that. As a matter of fact, the Bible says quite clearly you should love others as you love yourself.

But be careful not to play games with your subconscious mind when you make those commitments, particularly in regard to personality and habit changes. When you make a commitment to yourself you decide on a change of attitude. In effect you announce to your whole being that you are going to do something which requires total attention and help. But if you renege on your commitment, in effect you prevent all your conscious and subconscious faculties from completing the task and render them useless. What happens then is, that next time you become excited about the possibilities of a project and make a commitment, your subconscious responses will be slightly slower and less enthusiastic than before. It is as if they remember the previous broken commitments, consider the new project may not be fulfilled and decide that full effort is not required.

If you continually break commitments you almost bind yourself totally from completing anything because there is no track record of success in your subconscious. The 'commitments kept' ledger shows virtually nil and therefore no effort from your inner self is expressed. That is why it is so difficult to remotivate ourselves and why affirmations and self talk are so necessary to overcome that initial strong resistance to create motivation.

Do not play dangerous mindgames that will

hinder motivation and success and prevent you from becoming all that you desire.

If it helps, make less commitments to yourself but follow through completely on even the most frivolous. It's not so stupid to start by placing your shoes in exactly the same position each night without fail. Do this irrespective of what time you get home or how you feel from one day to the next. As crazy as this seems it will actually increase your sense of integrity. You will prove to yourself that you can keep a long term commitment at the most menial level.

Experiment with other ideals and build your integrity. Then watch your motivational thrust rocket.

I am continually asked how to motivate others. One young man from a youth help group said to me, 'How do I motivate the young people I am supposed to lead?' My answer was, 'Show them you are motivated yourself.' So many of us want to motivate and encourage others, but do not set the example.

To motivate others we must have the integrity to demonstrate it in our own lives. And to motivate ourselves we must develop integrity by commitment and stability towards our conscious and unconscious thoughts.

Keep short accounts of your personal integrity. Treat it as your very best and trusted friend. Relate to it always with honesty and commitment and it will bring you motivation and success.

MOTIVATORS
- Maintain a deep personal integrity.
- Be someone you can admire.
- Do not play dangerous games with your subconscious mind.
- Follow through even on trivial commitments.
- Treat yourself as your best friend.

Take Care in Selecting Your Friends

Many times I have had my back to the wall with, it seemed, no way out. Suddenly someone pointed out the funny side and we all collapsed with laughter. In the process we were revived to fight another day.

CHAPTER SIX

Take Care in Selecting Your Friends

To have friends is a wonderful advantage. To have close, meaningful, and selected friends is probably one of the most rewarding involvements of life.

It may come as something of a surprise to include some comments about friendship in relation to being motivated all the time. So firstly, let me give a negative illustration. If you had friends who were always criticizing, complaining, negative minded, suspicious, untruthful and depressed, and they poured this all over you, what would be the impact on your life? I guess in a reasonable amount of time, unfortunately, you would become like them. Just as misery loves company and thrives on forlornness and discouragement, so optimism, honesty and trust thrive on their counterparts.

Consider selecting your friends with care and deliberation and rejecting those who are negative and unresponsive. Whatever you do, avoid at all costs being the top person in your group, the motivator and guru of the crowd. Always seek to expand your relationships to the point that you have to strive continually to make your personality and motivation better.

To some it may seem cold and calculating to pick friends on a profile selection basis, but on closer examination and thought you will recognise the wisdom of the process.

Why not prepare a profile of qualities for friendship? I do this. Let me share it with you.

Firstly, a friend must be honest in all areas. I'm not for a moment suggesting perfection, but I do expect honesty in dealings and relationships. There is no room for a 'friend' who tells you untruths or half truths. Honesty means open and frank discussions with feeling and sensitivity for the other person's situations and point of view. I have real problems with people who cheat on their spouses. I consider that if a relationship so close can be broken — for whatever reasons — then *any* commitment can be broken.

The type of friends I am talking about are those whose hand shake or quiet 'yes' or 'no' over the telephone means exactly what it says. There is no need for embellishment.

Secondly, develop a sense of humour. I like to think that I can see the funny side of a situation and that those with whom I associate as friends cannot only have a good genuine laugh at me but also at themselves. To look at everything with a furrowed brow and to look at life with deadly seriousness does little for the imaginative juices that allow us to enjoy living.

It seems to me that it is one thing to be successful and highly motivated *but it adds so much more to life if you can enjoy it as well.*

Many times I have had my back to the wall with, it seemed, no way out. Suddenly someone pointed out the funny side and we all collapsed with laughter. In the process we were revived to fight another day.

Good humour also looks for the good in others. It seems as if these two qualities are indispensable and those who can laugh are much easier to reason and work with.

Thirdly, choose highflyers. Here I am talking about those with empires in their brains. Not so much to conquer and possess, but to master, endure and overcome, so that somehow, in the process, others might be inspired and helped by what is accomplished and propelled to reach their own potential.

Highflyers are always talking up, always climbing, forever thinking of ways in which goals can be accomplished and always seeing goals that others cannot see.

Highflyers are dreamers, yet they have the knack of relating their dreams to the realities of the here and now.

They are usually hard drivers — more of themselves than others — and intolerant of laziness and small dreams. But they produce, they perform and they persevere.

Having highflyers for friends helps you keep the edge on your own life and challenges you against slackness and unmotivated behaviour.

Fourthly, be generous. I know many wealthy people around the world who have gained their wealth by honest hard work and good thinking, but who find it almost impossible to give to others. They may lend a car, a boat, a beach home, or any number of things that *they can call back or retain.* But to give in the full sense of giving eludes them.

It is these individuals who have a poverty of the spirit because they have not learned the truth that giving provides joy and blessing. Giving seems to have an effect upon our inner selves that allows us to enjoy life and its pursuits with greater capacity.

I have never met a truly successful wealthy person in any field, but who does not give, who is happy and who has the respect and admiration of friends and family.

To sum up, my criteria for friendship are simple but effective: (1) honesty, (2) humour, (3) high-flying, (4) generosity.

If you have these qualities then you will attract friendships and be a great friend to others. Spread your friendship through as many areas of society as you can and be enriched by the diversity of vocations and personalities.

Sometimes I go into the Outback areas of Australia by aeroplane, motor vehicle, horse back or even camel to savor some of the differences in people. I have never yet found I could not fit in. It was Paul the Apostle who said, 'I have learned to be content whatever the circumstances' (Philippians 4:11). Being able to shift on the social register, takes us to areas where we can view things differently or learn to appreciate and understand the struggles of others.

In a recent visit to the Outback with a few friends it was interesting to see these 'men of stature', sleeping on the ground, grinding through the incredible heat and eating with one hand while brushing away flies with the other. To me the real measure of a person in relation to others is the dignity he shows in responding to difficult situations. Select your friends with care. They will sharpen your edge in life and enhance your motivation.

MOTIVATORS
- Do not try to be the top of your group — expand your relationships.
- Select your friends for (1) honesty, (2) humour, (3) highflying, (4) generosity.
- Make friends at every level of society.

CHAPTER SEVEN

Operate Within Personal Time Tables

How often do you allow someone to interrupt your day with trivialities and then at the end of the day wonder where all the time went? If you feel you do not have enough time, you need to realise that you have all the time you are going to get.

Operate Within Personal Time Tables

It has often been said that time and tide wait for no man.

But many of us have been waiting for one another and for events to unfold since time began! We are always controlled by the late runners or those who just make it, and it seems as if we are continually adjusting our time frames to suit others. In the process we are ignoring or abdicating our right to follow *our own* time requirements.

It is almost impossible to be motivated all the time by operating within other people's times zones. In fact, allowing yourself to become a slave to others in this respect guarantees a mediocre life.

How often have you watched a whole family going on an outing waiting for the last person to get into the car? Some people operate, consciously or unconsciously, on a power holding system that controls others simply by their delays or continual lateness!

Many business projects have been started with a clean deck with all parties starting on even pegging to get evaluations, market forecasts and budgeting. Then they find that another group continually needs more time to finish. Through the process, everyone who has been working diligently to meet time frames, is held up.

How then can a person be motivated all the time in a world that is beset by delays, disappointments and broken commitments? The answer is to operate under personal time tables. That is done by creating a personal life style of promptness and fulness.

This needs to be declared by act and by communication. Show others *you have certain principles under which you work, and those principles must not be broken.* For example, how long do you wait for a person who has made an appointment with you? 15 minutes, 30 minutes, one hour? What is your personal time frame? I will never wait more than 10 to 15 minutes for anyone, unless I know in advance there may be mitigating circumstances. By waiting any longer I have disadvantaged someone else who has made an appointment and kept it. It is very rude to be late for an appointment, and it is very bad for your motivational thrust. If you allow others to control your time and fail to tell them, you are putting yourself in bondage and preventing the flow of motivated action.

Some people say they never have enough time, yet 60 minutes equals one hour, irrespective of who you are or where you live. *But it is the way that it is managed that makes the difference.*

How often do you allow someone to interrupt your day with trivialities and then at the end of the day wonder where all the time went? If you do feel you do not have enough time, you need to realise that *you have all the time you are going to get.*

Time, not money, is your most valuable asset and it is neither redeemable in this lifetime nor expandable at the conclusion.

Who would not give all they had for an extension of time on earth? Yet we treat the gift of time so badly by poor use. We waste it as if it were the cheapest and easiest commodity imaginable.

Keep a respect for your own life span and allocate time frames to do *what you need to do* as well as *what you want to do* and *what you should do.*

Recently I was asked to take part in a world-wide project that would take up my time during a five-year period. Certainly, the project was worth-while and would probably help a lot of people. But at 55 years of age they were asking me to trade possibly 20% of my potential working life for that satisfaction. On that basis the trade was not so attractive. I had bigger dreams and a different time reference which I considered of greater value.

Time must be considered as your personal property. Only you can withhold or release it to others. As the custodian of such a vast and valuable resource, you must allocate it wisely and well. Control on your time has a significant effect on your motivation, because it puts you at the helm of your ship. It is up to you to chart your own course and speed.

Write out a list of principles in respect to time and keep them as a valuable guide for progress and prosperity.

It is amazing to me how often people, who will not give cash to help a charitable institution, will literally throw away their life by giving away time. There seems to be no correlation between values and time in charitable work. Let me explain.

If you help a charitable organisation for eight hours on a Saturday and they make a very small sum of money, is that time value worth any less than eight hours spent on your vacation? Further, would you work for a commercial organisation for what was made out of your day of giving your time for charity? Of course not.

If you want to help some charitable organisation for a day, then go to the highest paid job you can find and *give away* your wages! Then relax in the knowledge you have not cheated on the value of the time allotted to you.

Long coffee breaks, lingering lunches, wandering around the office, too much small talk, accepting unnecessary delays, and just plain wasting time are thieves in your life and restrict your motivation.

Also avoid others imposing their time frames on you. Watch this point with diligence and you will be amply rewarded.

Operating within personal time tables keeps you up to scratch because as you work within your own time principles you have the knowledge, responsibility and security that stimulates motivation and confidence. Working within those time tables also creates tremendous energy reserves. This is because you cut out waste and find you have more time for the job and greater concentration.

What a pity it would be if you continually tried to fit into other people's time schedules or worked out a time frame of values for your personal life — and adhered to them — but gave no time to loved ones and others. A time value system would not be complete without including other people — it is another of life's great investments. This is because as we relate to others with affection and consideration so we relate to our own needs and aspirations.

Operate under personal time tables to conserve energy, get more done, become more efficient and gain prosperity. In so doing you will find it almost impossible not to be motivated all the time.

MOTIVATORS

- Don't allow other people's schedules to control you.
- Remember time is your most valuable asset.
- Keep a respect for your own life span.
- Allow time for others.
- Remember — you've got all the time you're going to get.

Minimise People Dependency

I try and cut out the waste and ring direct, answer direct, respond direct and encourage direct communication and minimise people dependency.

CHAPTER EIGHT

Minimise People Dependency

As I meet dignitaries from various parts of the world, I am often amazed at how many people travel with them and are dependent upon them. It seems that as soon as someone becomes important or famous, they have a need to be surrounded by others as a confidence builder and insulator against the world.

While it is very necessary in some fields of endeavour to have aides and assistants, it seems to me that very often we overdo it, to the extent that it becomes almost impossible to survive without all those extra people. You finally become dependent on them and they on you. As a result the whole enterprise grows and feeds upon itself. It becomes a mess of overheads and committees along with a special pecking order which nullifies or reduces significantly personal and corporate motivation.

People are quite surprised when I arrive in their

country for two or three weeks with a medium-size brief case and a small suit pack as my total requirements. Not only have I found it helpful and necessary to travel with the minimum, but I find by travelling with carry-ons I do not have to wait around at airports, so I can keep a tight travel schedule.

Being motivated all the time tends to create principles in many areas of life and they do not always seem directly related to one's business.

To keep a tight reign on myself, I go through my wardrobe every 12 weeks and anything I have not worn I give away. I have very few personal belongings and need very few accessories to keep a business operating.

I remember well the very early days of real estate when I was working from one room at home with a telephone and a toilet out the back. How simple, yet efficient everything seemed to be and, percentage-wise, how much money I made with that low overhead. No switchboard operator, no secretaries, no counter staff or public relation people or any of the other trappings that 'typify' the successful business.

It was not that I was not successful. On the contrary, I was very successful under any criteria. I was earning and banking more money than organisations ten times my size. But it was all done with expediency and efficiency at a pleasant pace with dignity and planning.

Of course, today things are quite different, but at times I still reflect on those early lessons learned and the experience I gained, because the motivational thrust was in high gear while interruptions and distractions were minimal.

I am sure you have played the game of getting 20 people in a line and passing on a fact. By the twentieth person the fact is almost unrecognisable. *That is why to remain highly motivated we must minimise people dependency.* I am not suggesting we fire all our staff and go back to being a one-man band. Not at all, but I am suggesting the need to examine closely our people dependency and our people requirements.

It continually amazes me how often I am called by someone's secretary and then asked to wait on the line. During that wait my caller has become involved in another telephone call which means I am waiting till he is free so that we can do business. I try and cut out the waste and ring direct, answer direct, respond direct and encourage direct communication and minimise people dependency.

I carry a two year planner in my wallet so wherever I am, I can respond to any request on my whereabouts and availability. This speeds up and simplifies business procedure. The simple fact is that the less people there are in communication, the less foul-ups there are, and efficiency moves upwards.

But let's not confuse big business and big numbers of people. Consider this illustration. Some years ago I was asked to participate in a government enquiry into the possibility of increasing the number of small businesses in Australia. I willingly obliged, knowing full well that small businesses are the back bone of any country, and that out of small businesses grow mighty enterprises.

The conference room was well set up with a panel of people at one end. I was thanked for coming and then the premise for the meeting was again declared: 'An inquiry into how we can develop and encourage more small businesses in our country.' But before they could ask me a question, I asked them to define a small business for me so we could work from a basis of agreement to a practical solution. The question seemed to throw them, because they had never stopped to put a definition on a small business!

After a while they reached an agreement and suggested an enterprise of 20 people or less. I shook my head telling them quite strongly that their definition was wrong. They then asked me for *my* definition of a small business, to which I replied, 'General Motors'. They thought I was joking and reminded me of the thousands who worked in our country for the car making giant. I promptly reminded them that *big business is big profits, not large numbers of people.* I told them that the previous year, as modest as my business was, I made more profits than General Motors because they made a loss! If they kept going in that direction, they would have no business and no people.

Most people make the same mistake and relate big business with large numbers of people. Yet the highly motivated entrepreneurs usually only have very few people reporting to them. In fact, I know of at least one billionaire who runs his business with his wife at home, a part time secretary and a phone answering service.

Don't fall into the trap of expanding just to have the largest number of people on your pay roll. Rather seek out highly efficient and dependable people you can hire and through them keep your hand on the throttle. But whenever possible hold and operate the throttle yourself.

I have a friend who runs a highly successful world-wide enterprise. He has a very interesting system for minimizing people dependency. Once a year he spends a whole day from breakfast to late in the evening with each of his top six executives individually. They enjoy breakfast together and my friend asks each one in which areas and under what circumstances he feels he has not performed during the previous twelve months. He also asks how they could have worked together to reach common goals.

My friend is always cordial, warm and encouraging and his attitude is such that he always gets an honest response. All morning they discuss and deal with every problem area.

After lunch, knowing that the rest of the day is to be spent together without prompting but rather as a natural outcome, the executive usually asks my friend, 'In what area do you feel I have let you down or could have done better over the past year?'

This relationship of building and helping one another goes on well into the night and has kept my friend on top of a very large organisation for more than 25 years.

What is the thread that runs through this whole chapter? Certainly not to reduce the size of your dreams or the size of your existing enterprise. No, it is to examine your business style and find areas where you may have maximized the number of people to the point where you have minimized efficiency.

Hit the bottom line and go for simplicity. Have clarity of all levels and relate to those who have the answers or can say yes or no. In the process you will find your motivation increased.

MOTIVATORS
- Examine your people dependency.
- Go for profits not for size.
- Relate to the few who control the many.
- Communicate with those who can say yes or no.

CHAPTER NINE

Remain in Control all the Time

Your commitment towards your own plan is far higher and more determined once you have control. There is little commitment to someone else's plan under someone else's control.

Remain in Control all the Time

If you are to become and remain a highly motivated individual then you must at all times remain in control.

I am not talking about dominating the lives of others, but I am suggesting a principle of control over your *own* destiny. We are talking about the continual confidence that you are in control and therefore you can change — it also means that others do not have control over you.

Although much easier said than done, remaining in control all the time can be a principled lifestyle with guides and directions. Control does not mean holding everything tight or never trusting or allowing others to become involved. It is setting the principles of direction and response, allowing a free flow of initiatives with pre-determined guidelines.

I recall hearing how Artistotle Onassis, in the middle of the night once crawled over the ships that were being built for him. Dressed in overalls and with a torch in his hand, the Greek tycoon inspected and observed everything, ready to ask those important questions of the ship builders the next day.

He did not *build* the ships, but as the customer and owner, he never lost his perspective that he was *in control* and that any mishap or difficulty would finally find its way to his door.

Control means following your plan and time table and not deserting your authority as leader of your own life.

Dr. Robert Schuller says, 'Never surrender your leadership' because leadership of one's life and control of one's destiny before God is a sacred and solemn accountability factor.

Dr. John Haggai once said to me, 'As long as God gives me breath and my name is on the letterhead, I must exercise my chartered control.' Both of these men have demonstrated time and again the heaviness and weariness of control but that has never dampened their enthusiasm or efforts. Rather it has sharpened their motivation and skill.

To remain in control all the time means paying special attention to contracts, partnerships, laws and small details. If you don't, you will find that someone or some organisation will take you down a path that you do not want to go.

Accepting control means looking to the future and anticipating events by preparing thoughtfully for them. It doesn't mean explaining what you presumed happened after the event! To leave control of your life to someone else or to the whims of circumstances or events will guarantee low motivation and low commitment. Your commitment towards your own plan is far higher and more determined once you have control. There is little commitment to someone else's plan under someone else's control.

Be very wary of changing markets or variations of direction that may rob you of control. A seemingly slow crawl of events can take over without notice or a sudden shift of circumstances may take you by surprise.

In my book *How to Handle a Major Crisis* I talk about the necessity of financial reserves, friends and time and of remaining in control during a crisis. Likewise, I would suggest a principle of building into your lifestyle those checkpoints and reserves to enhance control.

Plot your course, examine your moves, relate to a set of proven control principles and the result will be peace of mind, progress and prosperity.

What then is wrong with following someone else's plan and becoming a small part of a big picture rather than the major part of a small venture? Should this present motivational problems? No, not really, as long as you have control within your work parameter. Being in control does not mean absolute control of everything. *But it*

*does mean being in control of that to which you
have committed yourself.*

For instance, if you are given control over a
project with an agreed budget, but do not have
the right to hire and fire, then obviously you do not
have control. If you have been charged with the
completion of a venture, but you have to repeatedly request permission to move ahead — or
are given unrelated responsibilities along the
way without the right of refusal — you are not in
control.

Also remember, if you want someone else to be
motivated then you must be prepared, within
agreed guidelines, to give responsibility to those
others allowing them to stretch and grow. I have
always allowed responsibilities over the years
and been careful with guidelines that to this day I
cannot think of one instant where it has not
motivated the person involved. It has always
expanded their capacity.

Motivation is made up of many components and
one of those very important parts is *remaining in
control all the time.* Within the control factor
comes the full commitment of self, and when you
have that kind of commitment you have the best
possibilities for motivation.

MOTIVATORS

- Control means you can change (any time).
- Control means not being manipulated or frustrated by people or events.
- Control means following an agreed plan.
- Control means authority.

CHAPTER TEN

Accept Total Personal Responsibility

It is sometimes said that most business people and entrepreneurs have their offices overlookng a busy intersection because they want to look down at the traffic and see something moving that they do not have to push!

Accept Total Personal Responsibility

The first act of maturity is accepting total responsibility for yourself and your actions.

How can we expect to be motivated all the time unless we accept responsibility for our good or bad behaviour? How can we expect others to trust us if we cannot or will not accept total personal responsibility? It seems to me that if we expect others to accept us as dependable and to put their welfare in our hands, then we cannot refuse to accept total responsibility.

My office seems to be a Mecca of people seeking help. They have trusted someone or some organisation with their money and it has been lost. There has been no accountability or responsibility.

Many times I ask the question, 'Did you ask to see the personal track record of success?' Always the answer is no. *Why do we continually place*

confidence in people or organisations without first
examining their responsibility factor?

I think part of the answer lies in the fact we *want*
to believe that someone, anyone, might have a
higher level of responsibility than we ourselves.
While there may be reasons from time to time for
difficulties and even calamities, we must remain
motivated towards correcting the situation or
even salvaging what we can. Then full and
complete responsibility is accepted and acknow-
ledged.[1]

If the Bible and the Christian Church teach
anything, it is personal accountability. Through
our lives, we are responsible for what we do or
what we are involved with, and one day we will
give an account to God for it.

If God holds us accountable, even to the point of
accepting salvation through Jesus Christ, then
how can we do less with ourselves and our fellow
man?

Accepting total personal responsibility in-
cludes our motivational level and how we encourage and maintain it.

What is our library of motivational tapes and
books like? How often do we listen to them or read
the books? Do we underline principles as we read
and listen and integrate them in our lives? How
much do we spend a year on motivation? The
average person spends a lot less on motivational
material in a year than he would on haircuts, and

then wonders why he is unsuccessful!

W. Clement Stone tells me that to be motivated all the time you must spend time alone each day to program your life and stimulate motivation. He also says that verbal and internal affirmations, before making a sale or presentation, create a motivational emphasis that propels you forward and helps you overcome rejection.

It is sometimes said that most business people and entrepreneurs have their offices overlookng a busy intersection because they want to look down at the traffic and see something moving that they do not have to push!

If we believe that motivation is a key element to success and achievement, then we should pay more attention to it by accepting the personal responsibility of increasing it. Consider spending a minimum of five percent of your total income on good books, seminars, tapes, videos and other motivational aids. Even try taking a person you admire out to lunch. Be creative, but be responsible.

In my book *How to Be Happy Though Rich* I emphasise and give a formula for measuring every day so that at the end of each day I can evaluate with some accuracy what kind of performance I have had and what areas I need to strengthen. Instead of just referring to your day as good, bad, terrific, indifferent and so on, why not develop a formula for measuring every day and

so lift your motivation and performance consider-
ably?

In accepting total responsibility for our motivation, attention must be given to health, and some
study must be made of our personal metabolism.
Without exception, I find that those who are highly
motivated are energetic and vibrant, even if they
are restricted by some serious physical impair-
ment. Actually, *you can increase your mental
motivation by physically acting motivated*, just as
you can find it difficult to remain physically
inactive with a highly motivated mind.

Many people suffer from poor motivation because they try to copy someone else's type of
motivation like staying up late or getting up early,
without paying any attention to their own particular needs. Often I have found that some who are
really struggling to achieve a motivated lifestyle
are actually fatigued and need more rest or sleep
than others.

Being highly motivated must not be related to
back slapping, loud talk, or super-active behaviour. There are many highly motivated people
who are quiet and reserved, but they get the job
done. After all, this is not an Olympic Games
contest for endurance and activity, but rather a
stimulation for achievement and success in reach-
ing your full potential which can be achieved in a
variety of ways.

One final aspect of accepting responsibility for

your own motivation means you must be willing to confront situations, people, obstacles, challenges and rejections, even if you would prefer to avoid them!

By being responsible for yourself you will be in a key position to accept responsibility for others, and their trust in you will be well founded.

MOTIVATORS
- If you cannot act responsibly for yourself how can you be trusted by others?
- Responsibility means confrontation.
- The key to Christian teaching is personal responsibility
- Total responsibility means measuring your achievement quotient.

1. See *How To Handle a Major Crisis*, by the author.

Make Motivation a Habit

Motivation can be activated and made a permanent part of your life simply by creating a habit that will last you a lifetime.

CHAPTER ELEVEN

Make Motivation a Habit

A habit formed is hard to break. This means, of course, that it can be used as a tool to motivation if understood and used in a positive way.

A habit is an automatic way of doing things, whether conscious or unconscious. For example, shaving, eating, drinking and toileting.

To be able to put a motivational habit into automatic control would put you light years ahead in your motivational quest.

I recall once arriving home alone and looking through the house. I saw a litter of bits and pieces of clothing, paper, packages and other items that I had left scattered around. The truth hit me and I realised that in business and public life I kept things neat, tidy and well ordered, but that here in my private life I had slipped into a habit of sloppiness, carelessness and dependency. I had expected and received a 'pick-up' program after me which had been operating for 20 years.

I became so ashamed of my behaviour that when my wife Robina came home I sat her down in a chair (I didn't want her to get into shock) and told her that as long as I live she will never have to pick up or tidy up after me again. And she has never had to.

How did it happen? I changed the same way as you can. I instituted what I call *habit force* and it works this way.

Some weeks after making my commitment to Robina, all was going well until I arrived at my office one morning (at this time I lived about an hour's drive away). I was about to go into the door when I realised that I had left my pyjama trousers on the floor of the bathroom at home. Now here is the key by which the whole principle is activated: *Never let an exception occur.*

Instead of going into my office, I drove all the way back home and put my pyjamas in the laundry basket. Of course Robina said all I had to do was phone her and she would have understood. But that would have destroyed my personal accountability and broken the principle of habit force. Of course I had the problems that day of apologising to clients and rearranging schedules, but *I kept my commitment to change my problem into a profit by making this cure permanent.*

Even to this day, I still never leave anything untidy or lying around because I have a permanent corrective system called habit which as a matter of course does the job.

Simple isn't it? Yes, and very effective. Why not substitute, as I have often done, the principle of instituting habit force? Motivation can be activated and made a permanent part of your life simply by creating a habit that will last you a lifetime.

What happens when you renege on your habit commitments is that you are programming your subconscious to expect failure. If that is how you program it, then that is what you will get.

Down to business: list the bad habits you would like to program out and substitute them with good and productive habits. Be careful not to allow an exception to occur.

Always be objective and do not make changes that confuse activity with objectivity.

Take care to analyze those habits that will definitely, surely and concretely produce the desired results. Do not go for those that may sound or look good and have little to do with producing the habit lifestyle you need.

Here are some tips to consider for new habit behaviour:

1. *Always be on time.*
2. *Do the important and productive things first.*
3. *Look for principles and key factors in every important discussion.*
4. *Examine, inquire and establish the real objective.*

5. *Finish whatever you start, and as soon as is practicable.*
6. *Stay calm and objective in all circumstances.*
7. *Continually upgrade your mind.*

With these, and other combinations for creating a motivated lifestyle, you can literally change your life by changing your habits. And once a good habit has been formed, it is just as hard to break as any bad habit.

Start off with something small when you want to create or change a habit. The discipline involved and the alertness required will be far greater than you first imagined because you have to put into reverse the existing situation. And on top of that, you have to institute something alien.

Don't give up if at first you don't succeed! Start again, again and again until you make the old habit redundant and the new habit part of yourself.

Habit-forming physical exercise is one of the easiest, because it can be routine and positioned before or at the end of the day. But remember physical exercise will only put you in better shape to get the job done. It will not get the job done for you.

Seek deliberately to create habits that are going to contribute directly to getting you where you want to go and doing what you want to do.

Make your motivational principles a habit as others have done and observe how someone will come up to you some day and say: 'You seem to be motivated all the time — how do you do it?'

MOTIVATORS

- Institute habit force and move into automatic control.
- Remember never to let an exception occur.
- Be objective — do not confuse activity with objectivity.
- Don't give up: try again, again and again.

CHAPTER TWELVE

Aspire to Something Greater than Yourself

If you want to be motivated all the time, then a magnificent obsession is what you need.

CHAPTER TWELVE

Aspire to Something Greater than Yourself

You will find the great people of the world aspire to great things and have a very in-depth, far-reaching perspective of who they are and what their role is in this life. Winston Churchill said, 'We are all worms but I see myself as being a glow worm.'

To be motivated all the time requires a grand view and a long term view of life and your contribution to it. Most of us with imagination and thought can create a light-hearted obsession. But it takes a deeper commitment to create and realise a grand, magnificent obsession. Mahatma Gandhi, Martin Luther, Hudson Taylor, Martin Luther King Jnr, Henry Ford, Roger Bannister and many others have paved the way, creating role models for us to follow. They also have shown us how it can be done.

World changers have big dreams and big ideals coupled with the determination and commitment to get the job done. I have never met a person who has big dreams, and is working toward them, who is bothered with trifling, petty frivolities or meaningless chatter. That is not to say that they are humourless. On the contrary, they generally have a very good sense of humour, but they do not dwell on the meaningless and the frivolous.

I was sitting one day in a coffee shop with my son Graham and we were both looking out of the window at the passing parade of people. I remember saying to Graham that it would be reasonable to assume that each person walking past was preoccupied with thoughts of buying a new car, paying school fees, clearing up the mortgage, going for holidays or preparing for retirement.

I observed that with the empire builders, from whatever low situation in life they start, their objectives and desires are on an entirely different plane. This is because they are committed to the grand obsession which controls their thinking. It signals their direction on what they eat and drink, how they sleep and work their way towards their objective. In this process, the normal things that others agonise over, are just acquired or dealt with as sidelines. Those things occupy minimum thinking time because of their place in the overall plan.

If you want to be motivated all the time, then a magnificent obsession is what you need. It will become an object of your motivation.

I suppose it is difficult for one person to give or suggest a grand goal or target to someone else. But I believe there are some simple but effective principles that can be followed.

Firstly, I believe for any great work to be effective it must have the realisation of permanence. To do something today that is made obsolete tomorrow or redundant tomorrow leaves some doubt as to the worthwhileness of a life commitment. Permanence leaves a mark or a foothold for someone to go further.

To do that which has permanence does not mean that it must endure the ravages of the elements. But in science, mathematics, medicine, education, industry, politics, religion and many other areas it may be possible to develop or create a new bench mark of discovery. This will create a challenge that provides a stepping stone for present and future generations. Columbus, Galileo, Newton, Einstein, Churchill, Billy Graham and others have created a permanence in their relevant fields that has changed the course of history.

The second principle seems to be that a magnificent obsession must make a maximum impact. Sometimes this requires little, another time it requires much. In any event, the size of the impact may be felt or reported on a global basis. It is sometimes amazing how a grand obsession, after a while, tends to multiply and grow at such a pace that it can even outstrip the initiator's grasp and become someone else's dream.

The third and final principle is, it must affect people, and to affect people it must be of benefit to them. No one would really want anything less than to help others.

With a benefit to others displayed in a practical and believable form, you will obtain the power and drive to get the job done — and realise the dream.

During the creation and pursuit of your life's goal, relate to God's perspective and account-ability to keep you on the track. I find the biblical principles, and my commitment to Jesus Christ, the governing factor and the enduring protection against arrogance, power holding and situation ethics.

There will be times of disappointment, discour-agement and seeming hopelessness. But you will, in fact, reaffirm your magnificent obsession. When you feel small it will help you feel strong, and when you feel down it will lift you up. And, of course, when you feel confused, it will give you clarity and direction.

Make your motivation match your dreams.

MOTIVATORS

- Commit yourself to a magnificent obsession.
- A grand obsession has permanence.
- A grand obsession has maximum impact.
- A grand obsession is a benefit to others.

CHAPTER THIRTEEN

Always have a Futuristic Outlook

I believe that to be motivated all the time, although we learn from the past, we must focus on the future because that's where we will always be living.

CHAPTER THIRTEEN

Always have a Futuristic Outlook

At the time of writing this book I am 55 years of age, and if there is one thing I know that is an enemy to my motivation it is meeting with groups of people in my own age bracket!

People over 50, and sometimes much younger, often talk about the past and glorify and exaggerate its benefits and achievements.

I was there for some of the great depression and World War II before we had refrigerators, jet planes, air conditioning, micro wave ovens, penicillin, heart transplants and all else we take for granted today.

I was there as a victim of diphtheria and the lack of opportunity, and saw first hand poverty and the awful crisis of polio and other calamities of life.

I believe that to be motivated all the time, although we learn from the past, we must focus on the future because that's where we will always be living.

It has been said the only thing of permanence is change. Realizing the implications of that, we should take a very hard look at our attitude to change. I certainly believe there are some things that should never change — fundamental principles. For example — the absolutes of the biblical charter are enduring and final. But changes may occur in the practical carrying out of principles.

Why not then accept that change is inevitable and welcome it? But at the same time, we must hang on to and exercise absolutes within that change. To welcome change means a different perspective towards its coming. It will not come as an enemy, but as a friend. We will see it as a challenge or opportunity to be grasped.

Welcoming change puts you in the top percentage of successful people because you are not restricted by the status quo or bound by the implications of trying to stop progress. It may well be that you can even help program change, because there are many things that will be changed every few years.

Why not create or program change and be to the forefront at setting the pace and implementing the strategy? The implications of welcoming and being involved in change processes can provide a motivational permanence which may endure for a lifetime.

Just imagine choosing a field and committing yourself to a life time of being in the forefront of change in that area. The motivation that would stem from it — and be required from it — would act as an excitement machine stimulating others and so revolutionise countless areas of practical involvement throughout the world.

Being in the front line of change also gives you some responsibilities to control. It involves bringing something forward before its time and preparing the way.

I am not suggesting for a minute that we change for change's sake, or that we throw out the old and bring in everything new. But I do believe the inevitability of change can bring with it benefits and progress, and resistance just for the sake of keeping everything stable is pointless, even destructive.

The key is to realise that change will be made and not to fear it, but to anticipate and benefit from its coming. Some changes come and are virtual false alarms with the old tested and tried ways adopted again.

What we are looking at in this book is the anticipation and the using of change to improve or protect our livelihood. As a result we are positively motivated and involved in the implication of the change, whatever it be.

Your lack of fear and apprehension towards a changing world will allow you to investigate impartially the potential benefits or problems before it all overwhelms you. All great motivated entrepreneurs plan, talk and aim for the future because the greatest human success story has not yet been written and the biggest achievements are always in the future. By the same token every new generation has within its hands the power to correct the mistakes of the previous generation and improve the next.

Rarely does long lasting motivation come from what *has* happened, but rather from what is *about to* happen or what *can* happen. With long term goals, which demand a futuristic look, changes can be planned to suit circumstances and time frames. This gives benefits, both personal and physical. Point those who work for you or with you to the future and watch them fire.

It is impossible to motivate a young man or woman towards a new job challenge unless it is presented with a futuristic look. Likewise, to enhance and endure your own motivation you need to look to the future with plans, optimism and objectivity.

MOTIVATORS
- Welcome change.
- Program change.
- Control change.
- Lock in changeless principles.

Give your Motivation to Others

When someone says something will not work, offer them ten dollars on the spot to give you one reason why it could.

Give your Motivation to Others

To be motivated and enjoy the benefits of such a motivation can be a totally gratifying experience. So why not share it with others? There are many people who need what you can offer, and what you give them in motivational encouragement or principles will be repaid one hundred fold.

When you hear of disappointments or discouragements, make that phone call, send that book, take that person out to lunch. By encouraging others and by lifting their spirits you will inevitably lift your own.

I keep a stock of special books for such an occasion. When I hear of people facing difficulty I can send them a gift with a short motivational inscription which should restart the engines and let them know someone cares. It shows that someone has enough interest to relate to them — in a productive way. I do this for people I have never met and may never meet, and the response has generally been an acknowledgement of the great effect it has had.

As you increase your motivational output and move around in life you will notice that others will be automatically drawn to you. This is because by your very presence you act as a stimulant in their lives.

At speaking appointments I find many people who want to tell me about their challenge and progress, expecting and hoping I will in some way endorse, encourage or offer some fresh advice that will help their motivational barometers to rise.

While it is impossible to relate and affirm everybody you meet, try always to leave a word of stimulation that:

1. *Endorses what they are on about (if you agree).*
2. *Assures them of your confidence about their future.*

Many times over the years I have been helped and provoked by others because they blessed me with the right words and encouragement. It was like water to a dry sponge at the right time.

Sam Heyburn, in Brisbane, Australia, is such a man. He rarely leaves anyone without giving a confirmation of their value as a person and a challenge to become great.

Dr. John Haggai, to whom this book is dedicated, has (unconsciously I believe) done so much for all those he meets and works with by his sheer motivational uplift.

It is especially in the areas of leadership that motivational giving is so rewarding. Some use the positioning of authority to control and manipulate, but that is a totally selfish, domineering and destructive way to relate to others. Giving motivation by allowing others to share or totally receive the glory and victory is an extremely good way to pass on the gift of motivation. Also allowing others to have some involvement and planning provides a definite degree of motivation and encouragement.

Many will read this book and hopefully pass on the message. But there are those who will not benefit. *However, imagine, if you will, the kind of world we would live in if all mankind was motivated towards positive action.* Your motor car would be serviced promptly and at probably half the cost. Your phone bill would probably be cut in half because people would call back straight away. Your debtors would pay on time — and your creditors would not have to send a second account! Reliability and positive commitment would be the word for every occasion. Your attitude toward shop assistants, newspaper boys, garage attendants, receptionists and many others can help make the world more motivated.

Some simple principles of giving your motivation to others are —

116

1. *Never respond to a negative remark with a rebuke or criticism* — always respond by affirming the positive. For example, when someone says, 'Isn't it an awful day?' respond with, 'Well, it will keep some people indoors to finish those unfinished jobs.'

If you are told that, 'That Jonesy character is a liar or a cheat,' respond with, 'You are an intelligent person, what could you do to help him change?'

2. *Never agree with a person when they refer to bad habits as part of their lot in life* — encourage change by suggesting a method and time schedule along with benefits, and reasons for changing.

3. *When someone says something will not work, offer them ten dollars on the spot to give you one reason why it could.*

4. *Speak out against negativity and inactivity* — challenge cliches and inactivity and suggest positive alternatives and ideas for success. Be bold, with sensitivity, and assert the need for motivation as a strong antidote for unemployment, failure, dissatisfaction and mediocrity.

Make sure that your lifestyle demonstrates your claims. There are certainly those who talk about motivation and act it out like a stage play, but they rarely produce the fruits in their own lives. There is always the trap of talking the talk, reading the book, listening to the cassette tape and bounding around like an orangutan without producing the goods and putting the score on the card.

Do not deceive yourself or others by getting into a rut of dreaming but never doing. Even worse, do not expect others to perform through your principles and dialogue but be barren of any real results yourself.

Results are what counts and the better results, the less that needs to be said. Lift the load of inactivity from your fellow man by producing success upon success achieved the right and moral way. And in the process share with others the simple and profound principles which you have found have worked.

Why not make up a mailing list once a month of people to whom you relate and share an encouraging thought or a motivational principle that you have found helpful and workable. Your influence on others will be returned to you many times over, and on a black Friday or blue Monday you will receive a phone call or note that will elevate you when you most need it and help you to become motivated all the time.

MOTIVATORS
- Relate motivational principles to others.
- Challenge negativity and inactivity with positive suggestions and involvement.
- Remember — what you give in motivation affirmation to others you will receive back when you most need it.

Be Grateful, Not Critical

Create a formula for reminding yourself about the good things that are happening in your life, and use them as a catalyst to restart the engine and keep the throttle at high speed.

CHAPTER FIFTEEN

Be Grateful, Not Critical

To be motivated all the time requires a special type of mind set that allows for the free flow of ideas, acceptance, discipline and openness.

The one thing that separates the growers from the slowers is a *gratitude attitude*.

Being critical and complaining about any situation prevents correction and growth and dries up the enthusiasm that is so necessary for success. Criticism is not only harmful and degrading for others, but it has a very damaging effect upon the initiator.[1]

The Bible says all things work together for good for those who love God (Romans 8:28). Being grateful for what you have, rather than being resentful and critical, saves energy and encompasses an incredibly powerful principle.

In an interview with W. Clement Stone in the *Chicago Tribune*, he was pressed for a negative by the reporter who mentioned several things in his life that to others would have been hurtful and disappointing. But W. Clement Stone reminded them of his living philosophy, and that is, 'For every adversity there is a seed or an equivalent for a greater benefit.' And so *he sees only benefit from adversities* and, because he looks for it, he obtains it.

Many years ago, when I lost everything, I was busying myself with the next venture when a friend came to see me. He was surprised to see me pushing on. He said he expected me to be devastated and forlorn, certainly not looking for new ventures.

He asked me, 'How can you keep going? Hasn't going broke set you back?'

I replied, 'After a short time of accepting responsibility for my position, and having worked out my own stupidity and the state of my current situation, I realise that the only person who can improve things is me. In fact, I am in better shape experience-wise and therefore it will be easier the second time round.'[2]

Being grateful for health, strength, opportunities and abilities gives you a cutting edge and creates a motivational thrust. We are what we have accepted or made of our circumstances, and to give up at any time while we have breath in our lungs is to accept total defeat — and total defeat really means death of the spirit.

The sweet, sure acceptance and inducement of

being grateful acts as an encouragement to others and gives you the kind of self respect you need. Go for a walk in the beautiful libraries and art galleries and botanical gardens in your city and savor the beauty and inspiration from them. Realise that you as a tax-paying citizen helped create such a wonderful example of dignity and worth. During the process your gratitude attitude will rise and lift your dreams to a higher plane.

Being grateful during adversity will lift motivation. But remember it is just as hard to be grateful during the high flying times of success — which can, and will, drain your energy and sap your desire leaving you listless and tired.

Create a formula for reminding yourself about the good things that are happening in your life, and use them as a catalyst to restart the engine and keep the throttle at high speed.

But be mindful that your gratitude attitude does not become a crutch to lean on, as if to say, 'Well, I have had good success and now I can stop or slow down.'

Being grateful has within its framework some obligations, particularly in respect to those things that still need to be done. Wake up each day with an expectant attitude of what wonders and surprises are in store and how you can grow through the day's experience. To increase your motivational thrust consider what more should be done and use the opportunities of the present as a confirmation of what further can be achieved.

In my many years of involvement with business, lectures and the motivation of others, I have found some very interesting principles that do seem to confirm that gratefulness creates motivation. Those who are forever looking over their shoulder with suspicion rarely develop clear motivational attitudes. This is mainly due to the fact that they are forever searching and developing mistrust and suspicion *by expecting it to happen!*

Suspicious people are continually chained to that mistrust and never really let go, they never really give full reign to their ability to succeed. In so doing they limit themselves and cannot be totally motivated all the time.

Greed is probably the worst block to motivation — although it can, and does, very often motivate others to activity. The result is — alienation, power mongering and ultimately corruption.

A philanthropic philosophy or value system that benefits others as well as self will always lead to a satisfying life and a dynamic and continuing motivation.

Even more, being grateful for *other people's* success leads to a bond of friendship which in turn creates a climate in which good motivation thrives (Philippians 2:3, 4).

In fact, most people are so threatened by the success of others that when they meet someone who is actually grateful for it, they can hardly believe it.

Genuine pleasure in another's achievements — especially if he is a competitor — is one of the most exciting forms of motivation you can ever experience.

MOTIVATORS

- There is always a bright side.
- You can change any situation if you change yourself.
- Criticism is loveless — gratitude exudes love.
- Beware of suspicion and greed, the two enemies of philanthropic motivation.
- Be grateful for other people's success.

1. See *How to be Happy Though Rich*, by the author, Chapter Ten, 'Wealth means Criticism'.
2. See *How to Handle a Major Crisis*, by the author.

Remove Motivational Blocks Forever

I continued probing, examining and reasoning until, nine hours later, I came up with the answer which has provided me with an antidote to my problem for the rest of my life.

CHAPTER SIXTEEN

Remove Motivational Blocks Forever

We all have that nagging habit of avoiding doing something we should do. Or we continually do that which is not only non-productive but sometimes counter-productive or even destructive.

These irritants tend to bedevil us, causing frustration and despair during much of our lives. I had a particularly bad habit and it just kept pulling me down and destroying my self-worth. Yet I seemed powerless to control it or remove it until a trip overseas.

I was at the Los Angeles airport and I was snowbound. With most of the air traffic grounded, it looked as if I would have up to 12 hours' delay before I could complete my journey. I was frustrated and a little angry because I would have to make my itinerary tighter, and what in the world do you do for 12 hours in an airport? Robina wasn't with me, so I was lonely. I had no friends to talk with and I was thousands of miles away from home.

As I began to pace up and down like a lion in a cage I was suddenly arrested by the fact that I had a great opportunity. Here I was alone without any possibility of interruptions with comfortable and private time on my hands to do any number of things. Wasn't this the reason that I went to the public library in my home town — to think, to study, to plan and reflect? And here I had the same circumstances but with more uninterrupted time than I had had for years.

I started to get excited. So I proceeded to dissect and examine my biggest and most persistent motivational block. I knew it only too well, so identification was not a problem. And away I went.

I dug deeper and deeper into my subconscious and wrote furiously in an exercise book. I went through the usual excuses, shallow reasons and pseudo rationale. I carefully expanded each thought until I came up with what I knew was the truth and reason for the awful, gripping, motivational block. I continued probing, examining and reasoning until, nine hours later, I came up with the answer which has provided me with an antidote to my problem for the rest of my life.

That antidote found, and the principles applied on many occasions, has given me new understanding and control over my life in that direction for as long as I want it.

So here is the challenge for you. *Why not come to grips with your biggest motivational block?* Face it, dissect it, examine it, worry it, keep asking yourself why, why, why, writing down answers and measuring them, not against what sounds good, reasonable or even practical — but rather against truth and reality. After finding out the reason you do or don't do what you should do, persevere for an antidote until you find it. The value I was to obtain from such a quest can be yours. You will wipe out forever that which binds you to frustration, guilt or mediocrity.

There are of course secondary motivational blocks, such as problems you come up against now and then. They may not be particularly big but they are irritants that you would like to overcome. As these problems repeat themselves, *why not make a commitment that any problem presenting itself twice will be eradicated?* Find a formula for handling anything that presents itself as a problem more than once. In so doing you will remove those blockages from your life that prevent motivational excellence.

Beware of sloppy habits which tend to rationalise your movements and yet in the process frustrate you.

One of the major items of help to me, and I see it so obvious in other highly motivated people, is the ability to *routine minimum daily requirements.* These necessities should be relegated to the backwaters of daily routine rather than have to be programmed into your day.

I guess now you would like to know what my major motivational block was? It was simply this: Why, when confronted with several minor and major tasks, did I do some and not others? Why did I allow some things to develop into a large problem when I was aware earlier that it could and probably would? Why did I do such silly things as go to my wardrobe and select only two pairs of trousers for the dry cleaners when in fact I knew that three pairs needed cleaning? Why did I overlook, forewarned with knowledge, some potentially dangerous aspects of my business? Why did I blank out of my mind information that could help me? Why? Why? Why? Some were frustrations, others were serious, *all* exclusions were stupid.

As I contemplated it all during that day at the Los Angeles airport I sought, not a comfortable or plausible reason, but the real reason. And this is what it was: consciously or unconsciously, irrationally or rationally, cockily and humanly, I was selecting the tasks I needed to do, simply to prove my right to say no! I wanted to maintain the power of free choice which God gave to man at creation.

God has never robotised the mind of man, but has given us a free will allowing demonstration of our God-likeness. I was in effect exercising that right as continued proof to myself that it did indeed exist. In the process, strangely enough, I was making wrong choices. Even a good thing can be a motivational block, if we are not careful.

MOTIVATORS
- Turn problems into procedures.
- Eradicate repeated motivational blocks.
- Routine daily procedures.
- Do not seek comfortable, plausible reasons, but real reasons, for motivational blocks.

CHAPTER SEVENTEEN

Look for Mentors

Mentors are important because they are living proof that the difficult and sometimes seemingly impossible can be done and done very well.

CHAPTER SEVENTEEN

Look for Mentors

I suppose we all have been in the situation where we have examined the plans and then tried to put something together that we purchased at a hardware or supermarket store. We followed the instructions, as we thought, to the letter. But somehow we were unable to finish the job satisfactorily.

I remember a particular item that I spent hours on, only to find that I had screws left over and not enough parts! So I went back to the store to see the finished product and immediately saw my errors. I was quickly able to retrace my steps and correct my mistake and construct the item. There it was —the finished product.

I had a friend who was putting a model aeroplane together and somehow could not work it out, even with the original plans. But on seeing the identical model he was quickly able to complete the task.

It is the same with motivation and people, because although we read the books, listen to the tapes and study the manuals, very often it is not until we *actually meet someone* and observe their style and manner that everything falls into place.

It is not that the books, tapes and study manuals are unnecessary. On the contrary, if you didn't persevere with them you would not understand the principles. If you do not understand the principles then, when you see them in action, you will not recognise them for what they are or what they can do.

What many of us need are mentors — those individuals who have developed and proven principles over many years and have demonstrated results. Mentors are important because they are living proof that *the difficult and sometimes seemingly impossible can be done and done very well.*

I find my mentors by reading biographies, which to this day occupies a very large proportion of my reading time. I try to imagine vividly I am with the person featured in the biography. Under that kind of relationship, I can, in some strange way, tap in as it were to the story, live it with all of its ups and downs, and under that type of involvement, benefit from the experience.

Mentors via books are very often dramatized which makes them appear to be larger than life. This tends to expand the awesome challenge of rising to new and unexpected heights in our motivational activity and resilience.

The interesting thing that I have found is that those who are famous because of their achievements, are often in the flesh less than I expected. Sometimes, I have even found them to be quite naive in some areas. But as I became better acquainted with them I was soon to discover their ability to motivate.

I have no doubt that to see the working model in action, or to observe personal performance and lifestyle through the written page, we can expand our own thinking and strive for our own achievement level.

Why not choose mentors in different fields which will allow for a more broad outlook towards life?

I also choose my mentors from those who are deceased, and through reading and studying all I can about them, I am able to create a pattern of principles that have been either forgotten or rarely used. Through doing this I enjoy the excitement of rediscovering something of benefit and apply it to many current situations.

Deceased mentors have some sort of magic about them. It is something akin to famous painters or sculptors. After their death, their accomplishments are seen in a true perspective.

Whatever your situation and whatever your goals may be, *you need to observe a working model in real life or in the written word.* You will find that others have gone through the good and the bad and the highs and the lows and still survived. They usually achieve with a surprising motivation that never seems to let them down. They are ever ready to snap into action at the first sniff of challenge.

When you are in a spot or need a motivational lift, consider your mentors. How would they react? What would they say to you? How would you respond to them? Even consider what effect it would have on you if you were suddenly in their presence?

My greatest mentor is Jesus Christ who gave us all, I believe, the greatest legacy in serving, sacrificing and winning for the benefit of all.

MOTIVATORS
- Mentors provide working models.
- Mentors confirm principles.
- Mentors inspire us towards challenge.
- Mentors show us the secrets of motivation.

Have Built-in Personal Incentives

What I find very interesting is that once an incentive is reached, then a new and fresh motivation occurs.

CHAPTER EIGHTEEN

Have Built-in Personal Incentives

We all work on an incentive basis. It is an absolute fact that without incentives we soon tire and energy is dissipated. Incentives can be in many forms such as prestige, power, wealth, positioning, compassion, love, hate, leadership. They can be tangible or intangible.

Whatever the incentive is *it must be for yourself* even if you want to prove by achievement your worth to someone else.

As a matter of fact, I cannot recall any incident in my lifetime related to motivation, that has not included some underlying benefit either to my self or to others. Men and women throughout the ages have been motivated towards a cause and that will continue just as long as mankind exists.

We all can be galvanized into action on any number of causes, be they secular, military, political, religious or commercial. History substantiates that fact.

Many years ago I was broke. I had failed in business for the third time — everything looked worse than black. From that position I needed some incentives to motivate me even though it seemed impossible at the time. What I did was to visualise these incentives daily and work towards them valiantly with deliberate purpose. In the process I elevated my thinking, style and behaviour to *what was going to be* rather than *what was*. The effect was incredible. One of the incentives was to buy, for cash, my own gold Rolls Royce for my 50th birthday.

At times, the reality of some incentives seemed almost laughable as I had to grapple with day-to-day existence and problems that forever plagued me. But I pressed on, believing that my incentive would provide the electricity to keep the generator going and it worked.

Before my 50th birthday, I owned the gold Rolls Royce, paid for in cash, and somehow it came, not as a pleasant surprise, but as a matter of fact. Most of my other personal altruistic incentives were reached as well.

If you want to be motivated all the time, and if you are serious about your life and will to win, then why not create your own incentive program?

Any incentive program to motivate must be treated like a goals program. It must be spelt out clearly with time frames and seen in total clarity. These incentives must not *take the place* of your major life goals program, but fit in with it. They should give measuring points along the way, like a school report card.

What I find very interesting is that once an incentive is reached, then a new and fresh motivation occurs. This stimulates our thinking and provokes us towards another plan and incentive program. Nobody will continue to do anything long term without reward. The Bible clearly states, 'Give and it shall be given unto you' (Luke 6:38).

Don't feel selfish or unworthy. Sit down and write out a personal incentive program for yourself and your loved ones and watch your motivation barometer jump.

Divide your incentives into weekly or monthly partitions for continued motivation, then longer for medium term and then, of course, much longer for long term.

Your own children, your staff, your associates can all be motivated by incentives, provided they fulfil their needs. *Incentives will motivate them to the desired action.* Why not have your own personal award program and pay up promptly on results?

Many years ago in our home, we had a simple short-term motivation incentive that included our whole family. It was simply this: As soon as I sold two or more properties in a week, we would all go into the Australian bush and hike, horse ride and camp. Sometimes this was just overnight, at other times for two or three days. But it was an incentive that we all knew. Every night when I came home I would be asked the question, 'Did you make it?'

Motivation itself needs motivation! A clear ethical set of incentives can help to achieve this.

MOTIVATORS
- Incentives work for others — why not you?
- Plan incentives to satisfy your own personal needs as well as the needs of others.
- Allocate incentives short, medium and long term, to give a continued motivational thrust.
- Use incentives to motivate your motivation!

Postscript

I have tried through these pages to share with you those things that are tried and proven by results. They have motivated me and thousands of others throughout all walks of life and in many countries around the world.

I hope you will find in this book the switch that turns you on to be motivated towards greatness for your own benefit and the benefit of others. This will endorse God's greatness and goodness towards you. Yes, you can be motivated all the time — if you want to.

NOTES

NOTES

NOTES

NOTES

NOTES

NOTES

NOTES

NOTES

NOTES

NOTES

NOTES

NOTES